Too Cute!
Baby Cats

by Christina Leaf

BELLWETHER MEDIA
MINNEAPOLIS, MN

Blastoff! Beginners are developed by literacy experts and educators to meet the needs of early readers. These engaging informational texts support young children as they begin reading about their world. Through simple language and high frequency words paired with crisp, colorful photos, Blastoff! Beginners launch young readers into the universe of independent reading.

Blastoff! Universe

Reading Level — Grade K

Grades 1-3

Grade 4

Sight Words in This Book 🔍

a	day	like	them
all	from	look	they
and	has	new	this
are	have	play	to
at	her	she	with
can	in	the	

This edition first published in 2022 by Bellwether Media, Inc.

No part of this publication may be reproduced in whole or in part without written permission of the publisher. For information regarding permission, write to Bellwether Media, Inc., Attention: Permissions Department, 6012 Blue Circle Drive, Minnetonka, MN 55343.

Library of Congress Cataloging-in-Publication Data

Names: Leaf, Christina, author.
Title: Baby cats / by Christina Leaf.
Description: Minneapolis, MN : Bellwether Media, 2022. | Series: Blastoff! beginners: Too cute! | Includes bibliographical references and index. | Audience: Ages 4-7 | Audience: Grades K-1
Identifiers: LCCN 2021001451 (print) | LCCN 2021001452 (ebook) | ISBN 9781644874851 (library binding) | ISBN 9781648344671 (paperback) | ISBN 9781648343933 (ebook)
Subjects: LCSH: Kittens--Juvenile literature.
Classification: LCC SF447 .L38 2022 (print) | LCC SF447 (ebook) | DDC 636.8/07--dc23
LC record available at https://lccn.loc.gov/2021001451
LC ebook record available at https://lccn.loc.gov/2021001452

Text copyright © 2022 by Bellwether Media, Inc. BLASTOFF! BEGINNERS and associated logos are trademarks and/or registered trademarks of Bellwether Media, Inc.

Editor: Amy McDonald   Designer: Jeffrey Kollock

Printed in the United States of America, North Mankato, MN.

Table of Contents

A Baby Cat! 4

Around the House 14

Growing Up 20

Baby Cat Facts 22

Glossary 23

To Learn More 24

Index 24

A Baby Cat!

Look at the
baby cat.
Hello, kitten!

Kittens have
brothers
and sisters.
They are born
in a **litter**.

litter

Kittens need
to stay warm.
They cuddle
with mom.

Mom licks
her kittens.
She keeps
them clean.

Kittens drink
milk from mom.

Around the House

Kittens love to play! They **pounce** and chase.

pounce

15

Kittens like
to climb.
This kitten climbs
curtains. Uh-oh!

curtain

Kittens
need naps.
They can
sleep all day!

Growing Up

This kitten has
a new home.
Welcome to
the family!

Baby Cat Facts

Cat Life Stages

newborn   kitten   adult

A Day in the Life

climb   nap   play

Glossary

curtains

pieces of cloth that cover windows

litter

a group of kittens born at the same time

pounce

to jump suddenly

To Learn More

ON THE WEB

FACTSURFER

Factsurfer.com gives you a safe, fun way to find more information.

1. Go to www.factsurfer.com.

2. Enter "baby cats" into the search box and click 🔍.

3. Select your book cover to see a list of related content.

Index

born, 6
brothers, 6
cat, 4
chase, 14
clean, 10
climb, 16
cuddle, 8
curtains, 16, 17
drink, 12

family, 20
home, 20
licks, 10
litter, 6
milk, 12
mom, 8, 10, 12
naps, 18
play, 14
pounce, 14, 15

sisters, 6
sleep, 18
warm, 8

The images in this book are reproduced through the courtesy of: Okssi, front cover; Ermolaev Alexander, p. 3; Andrey_Kuzmin, pp. 4, 16; Seregraff, pp. 4-5, 10; dien, p. 6; CebotariN, pp. 6-7; Lubava, pp. 8-9; Nataliia Iliuk, pp. 10-11; Teresa Jane, pp. 12-13; Tuzemka, p. 14; DenisNata, pp. 14-15; mik ulyannikov, pp. 16-17; Smit, p. 18; New Africa, pp. 18-19; Halfpoint, pp. 20-21; PardoY, p. 22 (newborn); Volodymyr Krasyuk, p. 22 (kitten); Africa Studio, p. 22 (adult); Varga Jozsef Zoltan, p. 22 (climb); Lilya Kulianionak, p. 22 (nap); Casey Elise Christopher, p. 22 (play); gowithstock, p. 23 (curtains); Rita_Kochmarjova, p. 23 (litter); Photo-SD, p. 23 (pounce).